27 Thoughts on Enjoying Life

27 Thoughts on Enjoying Life

Travis I. Sivart

27 Thoughts on Enjoying Life

27 Thoughts on Enjoying Life
27 Thoughts on Life Series, Book 1

ISBN: **978-1-954214-43-9**
Talk of the Tavern Publishing Group

Enjoying what you're reading?
Want a free eBook?

Go to
http://www.TravisISivart.com/FreeBook

27 Thoughts on Enjoying Life

DEDICATION

To those that have helped me by listening, and also by talking. But mostly to all those I love, have loved, and will love that fight this battle each and every day, a battle that most people cannot see or imagine.

Contents

ACKNOWLEDGMENTS

I want to thank all the great teachers that have influenced my life. Since my childhood forward I have had an ensemble cast of eclectic characters showing me how to roll with the punches, and when to stop taking a hit. From friends and family, to granola crunching bestselling authors, to scientific research, they have all helped me grow.

Thanks to Lee, Kat, Emma, Elizabeth, Richard, Angela, Tami, Markell, Chris, Kyle, Deborah, and all the others who gave input about their personal experiences with depression. A special thank you to Jody Neil Ruth for his blog and short movie, Demons.

27 Thoughts on Enjoying Life

FOREWORD

I have a good life and am usually happy, and I wanted to give something back. This book is a collection of suggestions which I have learned throughout my life that guide me and help me stay happy. Nothing here is new or revolutionary, and many self-help or "how to be successful" books offer similar suggestions. I especially wanted to reach out to people who face the daily challenge of depression.

Winston Churchill called depression the big "black dog" and fought with it throughout his life. He didn't claim to have beaten it, rather to have tamed it. I don't know if he specifically meant the following about depression, but he offered this advice, "Never give in, never give in, never, never, never, in nothing, great or small, large or petty — never give in…" It is great advice, and by never giving up you guarantee you will never fail.

I am not a mental health professional, though I have had some schooling in psychology. I am just some guy who listens a lot, asks a few questions, and listens some more. Many people have suggested I should be a therapist, but I have never felt that would be a good fit for me because I am too blunt and honest for most people seeking therapy.

I have never battled depression, unless you count having a "down" day or two. I have thoughts of my demise, usually a couple times a year. But those thoughts don't last even a whole minute before I move on from them, replacing them with more constructive thoughts. Though I am generally upbeat, sometimes I do have an "escape" day where I hide under blankets, sip a scotch, and watch movies until I am too tired to stay awake.

I have lost more than one friend to suicide from depression. I have watched my own mother battle depression and alcoholism, and never quite get out from under them. I have had friends that I had known for over twenty years, who always seemed happy and at the top of their game to the outside world, end it all. As I write this, I am worried about two more friends that I have known for decades who are battling depression and possible suicide. I don't know if it is normal to know so many folks who fight with this, or if depression is a common challenge, (if it is, we need a lot more attention on it) or if I am a special person to whom folks open up to with their problems. I do know I have kept more friends that battled this affliction than I have lost. So far.

I tell you all this so you know a little bit about who I am. I can understand the mindset of depression, perhaps even relate, but at minimum I can empathize. If you don't think I have the background, formal education, or right to talk about this since I have not battled with it personally... just put this book down and walk away. If you have already judged me, nothing I say beyond this point will change your mind.

While writing this I consulted with many friends who battle depression, asking for their input and what techniques they use to manage their condition on a daily basis.

I did not write this to make money; I will always have this available for free to anyone who wants it. I didn't write this to get attention for myself. I simply write this from decades of experience of helping those close to me. I say helping because, and I will reiterate this many times, I can't fix anyone's problems or fight the fight for them. I am only a coach, and you have put on the gloves and step into the ring. I will be here to give you advice, check your wounds, and wipe the sweat from your eyes, but you have to do the hard part. You have to fight this fight, and fight to win. You can never let your guard down or take a rest while in the ring, or you will get knocked down... and each time you get knocked to the mat, it is a bit harder to get up. So, let's get you the training you need to go the distance, and not get knocked down.

This book is not meant for those on the edge of a cliff, literally or figuratively, and preparing to commit suicide. If you are in that place, call someone. Now. Anyone. I will give some helpful suggestions after the foreword. This is the preventative and maintenance guide, not a one-stop fix-it shop.

No one thing will fix it. Faith, friends, medicine, and everything else are viable tools. They are all good things when used correctly. Find what works for you, but it is a combination of tools that will work best. Mental wellness is a journey, not a destination. It all starts and ends with you doing the work. Those other things can help, but you have to be an active participant. No one can do the hard part for you.

A note on medicine, get it if you need it. Don't feel bad if you need it, it is a tool to help. Talk to more than one doctor, research the medicines, and pay close attention to what changes with each modification in your meds type or dosage. Take an active part in what you are prescribed, you may not be a doctor, but it is your body and you should know it better than anyone else.

~Travis I. Sivart

Helpful links and sites for depression and/or suicide:

UK:
www.mind.org.uk
www.samaritans.org

USA:
www.agoracares.org
www.suicidepreventionlifeline.org
www.thesemicolonproject.com
www.yourlifeyourvoice.org
memphiscrisiscenter.org

International:
www.supportisp.org

1. Forgive Yourself

No one is perfect and we are all allowed to have bad days and make mistakes. You're no different. Forgive yourself and move on. Don't dwell on things that cause you to doubt or even hate yourself.

Allow yourself mistakes and bad days. You are not wrong or weak for feeling the way you feel, and many more people than you realize deal with these same issues. It is ok to not always be at your best, and you have to let yourself experience the full spectrum of life, feelings, emotions, triumphs, and failures. That is how we live and grow. But learn to let go of the bad stuff, don't let it drag you down.

27 Thoughts on Enjoying Life

2. Know Someone Cares

It is hard to see at times, but people do care. Sometimes it is the people around you, other times it is a complete stranger. But people do care about you and what happens to you.

Believe the people who tell you that they care. Allow yourself to be liked, cared for, worried about, or even loved. And also believe you deserve it and are worth caring about.

27 Thoughts on Enjoying Life

3. Baby Steps

Nothing happens instantly. Everything takes time. Especially when it comes to getting your life and your head straight. Some days it comes easy, other days it feels like it is a million miles away. That's ok.

Take baby steps. Little by little is a good pace. Let yourself build slowly and realize that every step is progress.

27 Thoughts on Enjoying Life

4. Laugh. Often, Openly, & Honestly

Many people would argue that laughter is healing, and some even say it is the best medicine. Now, I don't think there is any scientific proof of that, but I do know it makes you feel better. Allow yourself to laugh whenever you can. And not just ironic or sarcastic laughter, but good, full, rich, belly laughs if you can manage it.

Watch movies that make you laugh, watch stand-up comedy, YouTube videos of kittens frolicking, or whatever makes you smile then giggle, titter, and guffaw.

27 Thoughts on Enjoying Life

5. Shut down Mental Movies

We all have those mental movies. Some call them daydreams. Perhaps it is while you're standing in a line and someone cuts in front of us, you imagine how it could play out – from ignoring them to a witty put down, to a fist fight. It could be wondering if there will be confrontation when you get to work or home. Whatever it is, if it creates anxiety in you, learn to stop that mental movie. They aren't healthy and only lead to bad places.

Be a director for your head films and actively participate. If you can't shut them down – and most of us can't - try adding cream pies to them. Or squirrels, dinosaurs, famous cartoon characters, or whatever. Just change them enough that they are entertaining instead of trauma inducing.

27 Thoughts on Enjoying Life

6. Be There for Others

Helping other feels good. It gives us a happy rush knowing we did something for others. It gives us a sense of accomplishment and self-worth. Make it a habit to do this every day.

Say good morning to a stranger. Do something nice for them like open a door. Tell a coworker you like their coffee mug or shoes. Compliment people when you can (and it's appropriate) and let them know they are appreciated. You will make their day, and that can make yours.

Listen to others. I mean really listen, don't just wait your turn to talk. You might forget what you were going to say next, but that's ok. Most folks just want to be heard, not to get advice or input; they will let you know if they want more. And your friends always appreciate it when you're there for them. They have you as a friend for a reason, and that reason is because they like you and what you give them in the friendship.

Sometimes the best thing is just knowing you are not alone, and you can show others that others like them are out there by sharing pieces of you, even if it is via social media.

27 Thoughts on Enjoying Life

7. Physical Contact

Human beings are social creatures. Don't overlook the value of accepting physical contact when it is appropriate. A pat on the back, a handshake, or even a hug can help your mood a lot.

With those you are close to, initiate contact. Let your friends and family know that it helps. I am sure they will be willing to show support in that way also, and may need it themselves.

27 Thoughts on Enjoying Life

8. Don't Get Overwhelmed

One thing at a time. One step at a time. Both great rules to live by. Focusing on one thing and completing it gives a sense of accomplishment. It is one key point that any success guide will give, and it applies here also.

Trying too much at once, or even worrying about too much, can make the best of us become overwhelmed and shut down. So take it easy, focus on one task, project, or thing at a time. As long as you are getting something done, then you are making progress. A journey of a thousand miles begins with one step, and it is a lot easier to look for the next place to step than it is to try and look a thousand miles ahead.

27 Thoughts on Enjoying Life

9. Small Achievements

Relating to the previous chapter, small achievements are awesome! Allow yourself to appreciate and even reward yourself for them. If you have to clean your whole house it can be a daunting task. But if you start in one room, it isn't quite as bad. Or start with one task in one room. Maybe it is make the bed, or do the dishes, or pick up anything on the floor. It's easy to do one small task, and when you finish you can go onto the next task.

Appreciate yourself when you have a small achievement. Let yourself feel good, and even reward yourself for it on occasion. The real secret is that a series of small achievements leads to a huge achievement!

27 Thoughts on Enjoying Life

10. Lists

Got a lot to do? Make a list. If it is overwhelming seeing it all on one page, then put each task on a different page. Now break down each task. Cleaning the kitchen is more than one thing. It is dishes, wiping the counter, putting things away, doing the floors, etc. Make each item a part of your list, and check them off. This will let you see that you are making progress and accomplishing things without getting overwhelmed.

Lists also help you remember what is next, because it is often easy to get distracted and wander off. Speaking of which, that is another plus for the list, it helps you focus and keep on task. And when the day is done you have a physical record of your accomplishments!

27 Thoughts on Enjoying Life

11. Celebrate Small Moments

This is kind of like the small achievements I mentioned before, but different. This is not about achievements, but about life. Enjoy and celebrate the small things in life. This is living every candy bar or soda commercial you've ever seen.

Take the time to savor life. Watching a movie with a friend? Make sure to pause and realize how nice it is. Having a delicious snack or meal? Slow down and cherish it. Is the weather nice? Pause and breathe deeply for a few moments. If you can enjoy the small things in life, it makes all the difference.

27 Thoughts on Enjoying Life

12. First Things First

To accomplish things it is usually best to start at the beginning of a task. I know that sounds obvious, but many of us will jump right in the middle, and then have to back track. That can make you feel like you got less done because you had to do some things twice. Starting at the beginning allows you to see your whole project come together, whether that is cleaning up your home, writing a book, or putting together a multi-million dollar business deal.

27 Thoughts on Enjoying Life

13. Complain Constructively

We all complain, it is human nature. Some people don't know when to stop though. That can be unhealthy. If you feel the need to complain then make it short, to the point, and make it constructive. Have a purpose, and aim to find a solution. Then you are solving the issue and removing the reason you had to complain, which makes your life less stressful.

27 Thoughts on Enjoying Life

14. Mental Spiral to Chemical Imbalance

Science shows that when we're happy our brain produces certain chemicals. And when we're unhappy, angry, worried, or whatever, our brain produces different chemicals. Some people have the extra challenge in their life of their brains naturally producing extra chemicals of the second type. But the point of this chapter is to not encourage those thoughts that create those chemicals. I know that is easier said than done, but so is everything in this book. This is a daily fight, and it isn't easy, but you can do it.

When feeling that negative spiral coming on it is time to find something else to think about.

27 Thoughts on Enjoying Life

15. Do Things for Yourself

You deserve a break today. Take one. Treat yourself to something once in a while. If you can't afford much, then find something you like that you can afford. That might be tasty snack, a good movie, or just an afternoon nap. You deserve rewards for all the hard work you do; let yourself have it.

Treat yourself well. Shower every day, brush your hair and teeth even if you don't have to or don't feel like it, because we feel better when clean. Dress to impress yourself. Don't worry about others. It makes you feel good to look good. And if you feel good about yourself others will notice and be impressed also.

If we can't be good to ourselves, how can we be good for others?

27 Thoughts on Enjoying Life

16. Surround Yourself with Positive People

First and foremost I suggest you surround yourself with others who care and serve your life. I wanted to put this as the first thing in the book, then decided other things should come first, but this is of ultimate importance. The people around you are your support, your example, and your lifeline. Positive and helpful people will help you stay that way also.

Don't keep the negative people in your life. This includes family. Stick with those that are healthy to you. Negative people who are always complaining, using people, or putting others down cause anxiety and stress, which isn't good for you. Don't keep them in your life. If you must deal with them because of a job or whatever, then keep them at arm's length and deal with them only when you need to do so.

27 Thoughts on Enjoying Life

17. Eat Better

I am not going to tell you to diet. I am only going to say to eat better foods. Less processed crap, and keep fast food and junk food to a minimum. Use them as treats if you like, but don't make them a regular diet. Consider a daily multivitamin. Certain vitamins such as vitamin D, B12, B6, and fish oil are said to help our moods. Consult a doctor for more information, and remember too much of anything isn't good.

Healthy food makes you feel better than junk food. The added bonus is that your body processes them better, and since your body is working less to digest, you feel healthier. They make you look better in the long run, and that helps you feel better also. Regular meals help as well, rather than eating at random times.

27 Thoughts on Enjoying Life

18. Eat Smaller Portions

Overeating is a thing we do. Very few people follow the recommended portion sizes. Try it. Eat smaller portions and savor what you're eating. Big heavy meals naturally make us tired and inactive, and that goes hand-in-hand with not getting things done.

27 Thoughts on Enjoying Life

19. Do Something Constructive

Get a hobby. Find something creative and constructive that you enjoy, and do it. Make it something physical so you can see the results. A few examples can be art, knitting, gardening, music, etc. I encourage something that lasts, and though cleaning your house can work in this instance, it doesn't last, which is why I suggest these other things.

So many of us make video games or movies our hobby, but at the end of the day we don't have anything tangible to show for it.

27 Thoughts on Enjoying Life

20. Pay Bills ASAP

Money and bills are a huge stress on our lives. It is a constant worry. Try paying your bills as soon as they come in. It removes that little bit of anxiety and lets you enjoy the day instead. If you can't pay it right now, then don't and put the thought aside. You can worry about it when you get the money.

27 Thoughts on Enjoying Life

21. Keep a Schedule

Keeping a schedule allows you to know when you plan to do things and removes stress. Also our bodies function better when we have a regular sleeping, eating, hygiene, and play schedules. Yes, also schedule in down time and play time, they are important.

Another good thing about a schedule is that you know what to do even on the days you don't feel like doing anything. If you work an odd schedule then plan around it. For example, always shower right when you get up or right after work. Always clean the house the same part of the day, again before or after work. Go grocery shopping on your day off, etc. It is a bit challenging juggling around someone else's schedule (work, kids, whatever) but it can be done.

27 Thoughts on Enjoying Life

22. Exercise

I am not saying you have to join a gym. I simply suggest you do some form of exercise on a regular basis. Take a walk, do pushups, yoga, ride a bike, or whatever. It doesn't have to be an hour long work out either, just ten minutes a day is better than nothing. It doesn't matter what it is, just find something you can do.

The benefits of fitness are physical, of course, but also mental and emotional. It allows you to focus on something and clear your mind.

27 Thoughts on Enjoying Life

23. Stretch

We spend so much time bent over computers, TVs, and so many other things. Hunching has become a way of life. Stretching is healthy and relieves muscle tension. Find a short five or ten minute stretch routine to work out tense and sore muscles. It is good for your whole body, and when your body feels good it helps your mind feel good.

27 Thoughts on Enjoying Life

24. Make an Effort Everyday

Try. That's all. Every day, just try. Put effort into something, even if it is just getting out of bed, showering and getting dressed. Other days you can do more. The days you feel energized will balance out the days you don't. Just make an effort to accomplish something every day. Never give up. The only time you truly fail is if you give up.

27 Thoughts on Enjoying Life

25. Learn to Do Nothing

This is a tough one to learn. Doing nothing is an art the Italians excel at. That is not said snidely either, rather I say it with admiration. It is an art form to do nothing.

Let me define that a little for you. Learn to just sit and relax. No television, no video games, no texting, or whatever. Just relax and enjoy where you are for one hour. Watch the world go by without getting caught in your head or having to have some mundane distraction to keep you preoccupied.

Camping is a great way to do this, but not everyone enjoys or can do that. Try sitting on the front porch, or even just looking out the window. Go to a park and watch the trees, people, and animals. It is truly a gift once you can do this.

27 Thoughts on Enjoying Life

26. Sleep Right

Sleep is one of the most basic needs, and we often don't do it right, or get enough of it. So many of us love to sleep in but have such a hard time getting to sleep when we want or need to. We just can't shut off our head and the thoughts keep coming.

If you have a smart phone or computer you can download an app to help. They play soothing sounds like rain, cats purring, or ocean waves to just mention a few. Counting techniques employed in self-hypnosis often help save my brain from wandering off and keeping me awake with worries. Try different things. And don't worry if they don't work in the first week, keep trying them for a month. If that doesn't work then try another way. Sleep is so important, and so many of us don't do it well. Time to reclaim it.

27 Thoughts on Enjoying Life

27. Now. Right Now.

One of the most important things is being where you are, at this very moment. Many people are constantly worrying about the future or are busy remembering the past. It is ok to plan for the future, but you can't spend all your time wishing it was here already. Same for the past, we can learn from it, we shouldn't forget it, but we can't spend all our time reminiscing about it or regretting what has happened.

Living in the moment means enjoying where you are right now. Appreciating what you have, or who you are with, right at this second. Savoring your current activity or place makes life good. Live what you are doing right now, the past is gone and we can't change it, and the future will be along soon enough. Funny thing is, once we get there, it is now. Live now, right now.

27 Thoughts on Enjoying Life

Author's Note

I covered a bit of this in the foreword, but thought I would expand a bit here. The reason I wrote this book was not for me, but for others. For all of my life I have known people who fight depression, and some of them are very good people. They are not weird, or different, not any more than anyone else. They range from kind and giving to self-centered and arrogant. In other words, they are normal.

These are my personal experiences and reasons for me being driven to some small action now. The first person I know of who committed suicide was a friend from elementary school who lived in the neighborhood I grew up in. He was in high school when he did it and we hadn't talked for around six years, so I heard it second hand. I also recall friends in high school who had depression and suicidal thoughts, not that they always go together. I had many friends, (male and female, black and white, gay and straight) call me to talk for hours when they were feeling too down or dangerously self-destructive.

But back in the 80's it wasn't addressed like it is now. We still had the "suck it up" and "tough it out" mentality. But we were headed into a very self-centered decade, the 90's. In the 90's you were allowed to be selfish, whine and cry to get attention, and many did. The ones fighting depression still weren't heard, not really. People thought they were like all the others, especially since people with depression don't tend to cry out much when fighting their demons. Rather, they timidly reach out when they hit a point where they have scared themselves so badly they don't know how to come back without help.

I grew up with an alcoholic mother who went from unhealthy relationship to unhealthy relationship. She went through the classic symptoms of depression, but she wrote them off as anything but that, even blaming it on menopause in the late 80's. I remember begging her to get help, any help at all, and her telling me it was none of my business and sending me away. I remember telling her if it wasn't my business, then I can't keep trying to help. To this day I have no idea if that was the right thing to do, but I do know it shaped our relationship for the rest of our lives.

In my adulthood I continued to have friends call me for help, I guess because I listened. Of course I often tried to "help" by suggesting solutions to their problems, but in time I learned they wanted someone to listen more than they wanted "rescued". And the ones I did "rescue" fell right back into their pattern. I learned that this fight was one they had to do for themselves; I could only support them from the sidelines and let them know I was there when they needed someone.

In 2009 a very close friend who I had known since 1988 killed himself after years of feeling so alone he didn't know what to do. He had not mentioned those feelings to me for over a year, and I thought they had passed until the police came to my door at 1:30 in the morning to give me the news. He had left my name, phone number, and address in his final note as his only friend or family. I still keep his phone number in my cell phone to help remember him.

It is now April 2015 and the year has been an interesting one. As the idea of writing this was brewing in the back of my mind in mid-March, I saw a series of unrelated events, conversations, and coincidences relating to depression and suicide drop at my proverbial doorstep, (including two friends unrelated to each other being hospitalized for self-destructive actions). It solidified my resolve and served as the impetus of dropping everything else and writing this book.

Through the years many friends would call for advice and support. I would often voice the ideas in this book, ideas I use in my life to help me maintain a balance even in the stormiest of times. This whole book is my general life philosophy. I asked many friends who battle depression for their tips and secrets on how they handle their own black dog, and I was happy to hear them echo many of the things in this book. No one mentioned them all, but anything they told me they did was already in this book in one form or another. That reinforcement is what gave me the confidence I needed to put this out there for others.

If this book with its simplistic ideas can help one person in any way, then I am relieved that I published it. Not happy or proud, because this isn't about me. I will just be relieved that someone found something here that helped them.

~Travis I. Sivart

27 Thoughts on Enjoying Life

Enjoying what you're reading?
Want a free eBook?

Go to
http://www.TravisISivart.com/FreeBook

27 Thoughts on Enjoying Life

ABOUT THE AUTHOR

Travis I. Sivart lives in a state of constant flux between Richmond, VA and Washington, DC with his son and cats. He is not just an author but also father, public speaker, cook, pipe smoker, cat & squirrel lover, internet radio host, and so much more.

Travis I. Sivart is a Jack-Of-All-Trades. He has worked in mundane jobs such as restaurants, retail, construction, DMV, Notary, tech help, and more as well as more exotic trades such as; singing pirate, exorcist and paranormal researcher, Duke, cigar and pipe connoisseur, master of dungeons, a knight, therapist, minister, and has degrees in religion and metaphysics.

Travis I. Sivart writes Steampunk, Social DIY, Science Fiction, Medieval Fantasy, Young Adult, Speculative Fiction, Horror, and more in the forms of poetry, short stories in more than a dozen anthologies, full length novels, as well as editorials on manners, pipe smoking, and medieval re-enactment. He began writing in his early teens and his creativity flourished with the help of fantasy role-playing games such as Dungeons & Dragons, Marvel Super Heroes, and Traveler. He continues to craft lives of characters in the same worlds he brought to life almost thirty years ago.

You can find Travis at www.TravisISivart.com.

27 Thoughts on Enjoying Life

If you enjoyed this book…

Please let others know by reviewing it on Amazon or Goodreads, and let others know your thoughts!

Other books by Travis I. Sivart

Aetheric Elements: The Rise of a Steampunk Reality

Automatons and airships, bustles and beasts, corsets and curses, dandies and dastardly deeds, all await you as you explore the cultures which evolved into a Steampunk industrial civilization. An anthology of nineteen tales of terror, mystery, and adventure.

Steampunk For Simpletons: A Fun Primer For Folks Who Aren't Sure What Steampunk Is All About

A primer followed by a guided tour through the world of steampunk, from the basics such as where to go and what to do, to the aesthetic of the arts within steampunk.

Journal of a Stranger

The thoughts, ideas, philosophies, and inspirations of a time traveling adventurer. Delving into the psychology of man, life's eternal questions, burning passions, and the quirky pseudo-science of his mind, and more.

The Downfall: Harbinger

The Talisman came again, but this time it didn't leave. The magical emanations of the comet have brought terrors from the bowels of the earth and increased the powers of an insane necromancer. The chaos above brought out others seeking to wrest control of the land. Five people from different walks of life are thrown together by these events with the knowledge that the world as they know it is ending.

27 Thoughts on Enjoying Life

27 Thoughts on Enjoying Life

27 Thoughts on Enjoying Life

www.ingramcontent.com/pod-product-compliance
Lightning Source LLC
Chambersburg PA
CBHW031228120626
46545CB00003B/1032